The Other History

Scott T. Starbuck

FUTURECYCLE PRESS

www.futurecycle.org

Published by FutureCycle Press
Hayesville, North Carolina, USA

ISBN 978-1-938853-41-8

Contents

The Other History or How Federal
and California Politicians Killed Indians

A student in my poetry class says her history professor doesn't believe
Ishi's people were killed for 25 cents a scalp then five dollars a head

and such acts in 1851 and 1852 were authorized by the California Legislature,
reimbursed by the federal government, and celebrated by cattle ranchers.

I tell her there is no denying California spent over a million dollars killing Indians
whose descendants fight poverty with casinos.

I tell her the call number of *Ishi, the Last Yahi* on the 4th floor
in our San Diego Mesa College Library is VT 968, and booths are there to view it.

Later, I recall how the faculty parking lot overlooks Tecolote Canyon,
named after owls that, like the *Ishi* video, are mostly unseen.

Moon and Money Poem

Holding up a dollar, I ask the class what it is.

"Freedom," says a Tijuana student,
"from working in a maquiladora."

"Red money," says a San Diego student,
"if you see past the green."

"Cat food." "College." "A cheap prostitute."

I tell them to dig deeper.

"Paper and green ink."

Deeper.

"Dead trees and petroleum."

Imagine you are on the moon
and dig way deeper.

"Symbolism that represents
interests of the symbol-makers."

Good.

I ask who the symbol-makers are
but no one answers.

Flipping the bill,
I end with four treasonous questions:
"Who commissioned this pyramid?"
"Who built it?"
"Barring wages, what was promised
and actually paid?"

History Teacher

looks over the class,
sees wet clay
and fossil ribs.

A hand shoots up
like Chartres Cathedral.
He answers.

"Once, I loved a woman
with green eyes
and red hair."

More wet clay
and fossil ribs.

What If One Night a Highly-charged Comet Went By

and everyone forgot language
so that no one could argue, buy, sell, cheat or lie?

All computer hard drives were wiped clean
and circuits didn't work anyway.

Starbucks, GM, GE, and BP were gibberish.
War, cars, radio, and TV were impossible.

Libraries were shelves of paperweights.
Laws and regulations were void.

Google faded out of consciousness
along with cell phones

and people began to mistake
fork-like cell towers for modern art.

Money, billboards, and sacred texts meant nothing.
Constellations guided travelers.

Terrified and speechless,
Congress and the President just sat and stared.

But sky appeared as always.
Geese, whales, caribou and salmon migrated.

Cougars hunted in forests
and bears ate meadow berries.

Suddenly, men had to listen in wordless ways
to women, stars, seasons, and each other.

People had vague memories of who they were
and where they had been before the comet

but no one could read names, titles, maps, or road signs
even though comics

and the spontaneity of dogs, cats, and children
still made them laugh.

Like after an Ice Age without ice,
everyone had to learn from scratch.

People noticed colors, sounds, and smells
outside in ways they never had.

Pine trees, like in pioneer times, became close friends.
Humans who hadn't smiled in years smiled.

People rose at sunrise
and went to bed at moonrise.

The wheel and sewing needle
became essential.

Doctors had to relearn doctoring.
Parents had to relearn parenting.

Farmers had to relearn farming.
Builders had to relearn building.

Cooks had to relearn cooking.
You get the idea.

Somehow artists and musicians
made art and music but,

because no one could read names,
their fame was limited to locals.

It was mostly unknown when
San Andreas Fault slid LA into the Pacific

and another tsunami took out
the top half of Japan.

When Mount St. Helens made Seattle
look like Pompeii

there were no advertisers, merchants
or media to profit.

The human mind changed in ways
that had been impossible.

Without countless pressures, distractions,
clogged airways, and moving images in boxes

people began to hear themselves
in green and blue silences

so that Taoist monks and tai chi
became the norm.

It was the worst time ever
for bankers and politicians

and the best time for everyone else.

The Dream of Greece, Wisconsin, and One-armed Trees

Our governments cut back trees to one branch
so we don't waste fruit on people and birds who can't pay for it.

Along with each branch there is a ribbon-cutting ceremony
for a federally funded tire swing
to keep the unemployed and their children happy.

Greek leaders say Greece is the birthplace
of a free and open democracy.

Wisconsin leaders say each raised fruit at the tip
is a torch in the hand of the Statue of Liberty.

Socrates says to never trust a politician.

In both Greece and Wisconsin, the common man is
an anchovy in a school of barracudas.

Somewhere in the night, a ball game is playing
on a laundromat TV

with two outs and two strikes in the bottom of the ninth.

The Builders' Sons Discuss History and Literature

I dream I'm in a posh London hotel where I work as a janitor
while the builders' sons are down to serious business
planning the fate of the world.

To them, the G20 Summit in Pittsburgh, IMF, World Bank,
US Congress, UN, and the Fed are jokes.

I sit under a table, drink lemonade, and listen to them talk
about a growing need for population control and
challenges from new builders' sons in Russia, India, and China.

"Hell, the 'Drunkards of Menkaure' enjoyed building the pyramid.
Their hieratic scripts reveal they made a game out of it" says a Luxembourgian.
"Shakespeare understood human power is always about human psychology."

"If that doesn't work, we threaten economic war
to motivate the uncooperative," says an Englishman.
"If they try to change the reserve currency too soon,
we bomb the hell out of them, figuratively speaking."

An American says "We start by convincing them the same way
Tom Sawyer tricked kids into painting that fence.
If that doesn't work, I agree with the Englishman."

I can tell by their conversation they are educated, and
most believe they serve humanity by ruling humanity.

"Pay no attention to that man behind the curtain," said the *Wizard of Oz,*
written by L. Frank Baum, whose father, Benjamin, many sources note,
"made a fortune in Pennsylvania oil."

Louisiana Agates

in burgundy, ruby, and moss
glow like pieces of broken sun
or rock candy
featuring ships in bottles,
crawfish, shrimp, oysters,
dolphins, sea turtles,
manatees, leaping fish,
and human faces—
all things that,
minus the lies of BP,
could still be today.

Patient Y

says he's scared of continental drift,
that some morning he'll be thrown
from his bed when North America
slams into Europe.

I do my best not to laugh
because his onion face is so serious.
"You really think
that will happen soon?" I ask.

He coldly says he doesn't know,
that he wasn't supposed to lose
his job, house, or wife
of 35 years either.

Before You Were Born

some computer figured
how many bottles of Pepsi
you'd buy
before you died,

how many times you'd make love,
throw dice,
eat crackers.

How many reruns
you'd watch
and watch again.

It wasn't counting
on you waking up, ever.

Remembering Kurt Cobain While Driving
Over the Wishkah River

> "[...] another third [of Cobain's ashes] were scattered in the Wishka"
> —The Aberdeen Museum of History

Given only two choices,
I'd rather be homeless
than heartless.

Listening to a Banker Talk About Losing [Only] Two Billion Dollars as Schools Are Closed

"Yes, JPMorgan Chase lost $2 billion in late April-early May trading. But last year, this bank earned $17.45 billion." —Rich Smith, *The Motley Fool,* posted at *Daily Finance* on May 16, 2012

It was a fish with the head of a lion
or maybe it was a goat's head
or maybe it was the head of a rhinoceros.
It's hard to say.
But it had fins, I'm sure of that.
So on Tuesday it was a fish.
By Wednesday, maybe it wasn't a fish.
These fish are like that.
Maybe by then, it only looked like a fish.
Like maybe, I only look like a banker.
Maybe I'm something else entirely.
Maybe.

San Diego Swap Meet

All Elvis on one table,
antique fishing reels on another,
blazing turquoise,
brass buckles,
knives,
old-time photos—
but it is the people
who interest me,
trying to make a few dollars
sitting all day
in a Sports Arena lot,
kind,
patient,
smiling,
petting small dogs,
eternally ready for conversation
about anything,
so unlike bankers
I heard testify
before Congress.

Deep in the Old Growth Forest

sunlight through cascading pools
says getting mad at politicians
who sell their souls
for women or money
is like getting mad
at an insane dog
who bites your hand
or a big tree
the wind pushes over.

For Uncle Ed

The sacred wildness is unlikely to survive

an alcoholic father,
the Korean War,

40 years in an assembly line,

and an inability to pay for a wife's
cancer medication.

But sometimes it does anyway,

as when an unknown vigilante
jumps a fence in the dark

and spray paints a fleet
of black and white police cars

blue
as a field of aster.

Ode to Milton Shinklebauer

"The Common Core State Standards in English, which have been adopted in 46 states and the District, call for public schools to ramp up nonfiction so that by 12th grade students will be reading mostly 'informational text' instead of fictional literature. [...] Among the suggested nonfiction pieces for high school juniors and seniors [is] 'FedViews,' by the Federal Reserve Bank of San Francisco (2009). [...] English teachers across the country are trying to figure out which poetry, short stories and novels might have to be sacrificed to make room for nonfiction. [...] Sheridan Blau, a professor at Teachers College at Columbia University, said teachers across the country have told him their principals are insisting that English teachers make 70 percent of their readings nonfiction. 'The effect of the new standards is to drive literature out of the English classroom,' he said." —Lyndsey Layton's article "Common core sparks war over words," *The Washington Post,* December 2, 2012

While we respect your experience, evaluations, and publishing record,
we must deny your inclusion of Chinese poet T'ao Ch'ien (365-427)
because his poems are not consistent with our goal
to develop "productive community citizens."
Surely, descriptions of Ch'ien's job as "a caged bird longing
for remembered groves" or "a pond fish dreaming of deep seas"*
are deeply offensive to our business community as well as
your colleagues working to prepare students for success.

As a substitute, we suggest poet Milton Shinklebauer,
who comes highly recommended by an anonymous donor.
Shinklebauer's sonnets of Ford's assembly line
and villanelles of Total Quality Management
have made him a sort of "capitalist Shakespeare"
consistent with our mission statement.
From now on, we hope you understand
free verse is out of the question.

* T'ao Ch'ien translations used with permission of Sam Hamill

Why Portland, Oregon, Should Print Money

"Portland[, Oregon]—that bastion of radicalism once dubbed 'Little Beirut' by the elder George Bush..." —"All Quiet in Little Beirut" by Amy Roe, *Willamette Week Online,* December 11th, 2002

"The SEC claimed that Goldman had failed to disclose that a hedge fund that was betting against the security had selected some of the mortgage loans included in the portfolio, costing investors as much as $1bn." —John Carney, Senior Editor, CNBC.com, September 8th, 2010

"Goldman Sachs agreed on Thursday to pay a lower-than-expected $550m fine [...] Although the penalty is the biggest levied on a Wall Street bank, it amounts to around a week's worth of trading revenues for Goldman [...]" —"Goldman Sachs settles with SEC" by Francesco Guerrera, Henny Sender, and Justin Baer in New York, *Financial Times,* July 15, 2010

"The Cascadia Hour Exchange has been up and running for about 18 years, but momentum has really started to pick up in the past year. Based in Portland, the exchange recently started issuing currency in Brookings on the Oregon coast and plans to expand to several other nearby neighborhoods later this year. The currency, called the CHE, is meant to facilitate bartering among locals. [...] The bills feature sketches of Oregon scenery like mountains and ocean, and each bill states 'In Each Other We Trust.' " —"Funny money? 11 local currencies" by Blake Ellis @*CNNMoney,* January 27, 2012

In 1970, the fight in Tigard, Oregon, looked hopeless for the little kid
until he caught the bully with a left hook to the temple.
"Kick," said my friend, Clay, staring at the chubby blue sweater
flour-sacked on the dirt, and we all knew what he meant.

The word "Kick" appeared again in 2007 on S.E. Wildcat Mountain Drive
when an Eagle Creek man helped three big pigs trash his house
after the bank rejected his loan modification.

My neighbor, who planned to fish Eagle Creek with me,
allegedly removed his electrical items, bathtubs, kitchen island, doorbell, and
    fireplace
when the bank refused to work with him.

Today, as I contemplate the SEC allegation that Goldman Sachs
allowed their client to cherry pick out the best-performing Wells Fargo loans
so this client could profit from a bet a mortgage portfolio would go bust,

I am reminded of my hero Jimmy Snuka's "coconut bop" all those evenings
on Saturday Night Portland Wrestling, the bad guys
Ripper Collins and Bull Ramos flat on the mat.

Thinking About Global Warming and the Orange Tree Outside My Kitchen Window

The problem with metaphor is
a painting of an orange
is not an orange.
Humans and birds need to eat.

Real oranges are suspended
like little worlds
on their long branches.

Pacific mist makes them glisten
in the morning
and the noon sun makes them glow.

When I was sick with the flu
my landlord brought me some
to drink.

Sometimes they fall,
turn orange-yellow
then red as Mars and rot.

Birds harvest insects
and seeds
make new sprouts.

The problem with metaphor is
a poem about the Earth
is not the Earth.

Poem Against Yellow School Buses

Someday, they will be green and blue as the Earth,
not social-conditioning yellow like yield signs.

The first thing a child sees in the Oregon morning
should be hope, not an overripe banana on wheels.

School boards will resist, of course, with cries
of "tradition, consistency, accident prevention"

but there are other planetary accidents
real as rain, or the lack thereof.

Antarctic Dream After Watching
Chasing Ice

The bumper sticker near the airport asks
"Are You Really Awake?"

As I fly south on Alaska Airlines Flight 529,
a kid beside me watches *Gilligan's Island* reruns.

I drift off, and the pilot announces
Amundsen Sea Embayment just melted

so during the trip from Portland to San Diego
the sea will rise 20 feet.

"I guess that wrecks my surf trip," says Gilligan.
"I guess that wrecks my ocean-front condo," says Ginger.

"I guess that wrecks London, Tokyo, Mumbai, New York,
Bangladesh, and the Netherlands," says the Professor.

And They Thought We Were Talking About Caribou

In the dream geologists report there is a 95% chance
of drilling 16 billion barrels of dinosaur blood
from the Arctic National Wildlife Refuge,
the land Gwich'in hunters call
"the sacred place where life begins."

So we drill and destabilize Earth's rotation.

Next, there is a massive pole shift.
The Pacific Ocean flows into Phoenix, Arizona.
So the Phoenix legend continues its circular story
until separateness is recognized as illusion
by some future remnant of humans.

How It Is

"For several days this month, Greenland's surface ice cover melted over a larger area than at any time in more than 30 years of satellite observations." —Maria-José Viñas, NASA's Earth Science News Team, July 24, 2012, at www.nasa.gov/topics/earth/features/greenland-melt.html

Sometimes you forget Greenland exists
like two pages stuck together in a novel
or a speed sign missed on a dark highway.

Then it melts and Holland disappears.
At this point everyone wonders,
"Will humanity survive?"

and I think of Butterfield Construction
when I was a boy, and how,
even in the harshest neighborhoods

with metal bars on windows,
words in concrete were mostly about love.

The Biker on the Ferry from Coupeville to Port Townsend

doesn't pray but instead
drives aggressively
because "No one gives an inch."

A pipe fitter from Scappoose,
he learned to survive
on the highway and off

like sea cucumbers below us
who expel their guts
and grow new ones

only after predators
have passed.

On the Ferry Between Port Angeles and Victoria

Someday there will be
no sign humans existed,

settled in coves
after an ice age,

plowed squares
for boxes to live in,

made art, reservoirs
or weapons.

But yesterday,
I gave a five

to a Native woman
holding cardboard

who smiled
like the red ball sun—

almost too bright
to look at.

Hiking the Superstitions I Realized

Oxygen is plant breath.
Paper is tree flesh.
Money is belief.
And no matter
what they say,
America is still
a stolen country.

Enjoy the Internet Before It's Over

"1910 Last salmon seen in Los Angeles River" —Patricia Dung, UCLA Science Project Co-Director quoted in *The L.A. Story Virtual Tour*

"One of the most commonly used [salmon] dyes, Canthaxanthin, has been linked to human eye defects and retinal damage." —farmedsalmonexposed.org

"The aims of the Encyclopedia seem harmless enough to us. But authoritarian governments don't like dictionaries. They live by lies and bamboozling abstractions and can't afford to have words accurately defined. The encyclopedia was twice suppressed [...]" —*Civilization* [VHS tape] by Kenneth Clark: A personal view (Chapter 10—The Smile of Reason)

"One leading concern of the Trilateral scholars was the failure of the institutions responsible for the 'indoctrination of the young'—the schools, the universities, the churches. They're not indoctrinating the young properly. That's why we have these uprisings in the streets and the efforts of the special interests to press their demands in the political arena. The Trilateral scholars therefore urged more 'moderation in democracy' if the national interest is to be protected, and more effective indoctrination of the youth." —"Chomsky: The Corporate Assault on Public Education: Our kids are being prepared for passive obedience, not creative, independent lives" from Part II of the transcript of a speech Noam Chomsky delivered in February on "The Common Good" and published at *AlterNet.org* March 8, 2013*

Before 1911, and the corner 7-11, salmon ascended Los Angeles River,
bringing nutrients from the vast sea to the Tongva and Chumash.

Now, gray farmed salmon dyed pink is sold by nearby grocers
while the canyon, like minds of TV watchers,

alternates between a sewer and a storm drain.
Nearby, a woman feeds stray cats a can of salmon

and half-remembers Joni Mitchell—
"But we're caught in Walmart's bargain."

We are caught in Walmart's bargain,
and our knowing this is dangerous to the money changers.

When Diderot's *Encyclopédie* appeared in France
between 1751 and 1772, the aristocracy was furious

because men, like those thousands of years before,
could finally make decisions
in their own best interests.

* Chomsky speech used with permission of Noam Chomsky

Why All US-Made Nuclear Waste
Must Be Stored at the White House

"The problem is how to keep radioactive waste in storage until it decays after hundreds of thousands of years. The geologic deposit must be absolutely reliable as the quantities of poison are tremendous. It is very difficult to satisfy these requirements for the simple reason that we have had no practical experience with such a long term project. Moreover permanently guarded storage requires a society with unprecedented stability." —Hannes Alfvén, Nobel laureate in physics, quoted in John Abbotts' October 1979 paper "Radioactive waste: A technical solution?," *Bulletin of the Atomic Scientists:* 12-18.

"Adequately managing these radioactive wastes for 240,000 years is, at best, a daunting proposition. The nuclear industry has already proven itself incapable of keeping track of its high-level nuclear waste for even 30 years. High-level radioactive waste has already gone missing from one, if not several, nuclear reactors." —greenpeace.org

"I am an FBI agent. My superiors have ordered me to lie about a criminal investigation I headed in 1989. We were investigating the US Department of Energy, but the US Justice Department covered up the truth. I have refused to follow the orders to lie about what really happened during that criminal investigation at Rocky Flats Nuclear Weapons Plant." Special Agent Lipsky quoted in *The Ambushed Grand Jury: How the Justice Department Covered up Government Nuclear Crimes and How We Caught Them Red Handed* by Wes McKinley and Caron Balkany

"As a physician, I contend that nuclear technology threatens life on our planet with extinction. All of us will be affected by radioactive contamination, unless we bring about a drastic reversal of our government's pro-nuclear policy." —Helen Caldicott, MD, at helencaldicott.com

Nobody sane wants it,
not Carlsbad, New Mexico, people,
not Hanford, Washington, people,
not Idaho Falls, Idaho, people,
not Needles, California, people,
not Paducah, Kentucky, people,
not Panhandle, Texas, people,
not Rocky Flats, Colorado, people,
not Savannah River, South Carolina, people,
especially not Yucca Mountain, Nevada, people.

Let those who benefit most
from defense contracts
have it all.

Immediately.
Today.

Eisenhower, in his farewell address,
spoke the truth
about the dangers
of the military-industrial complex,
but to whom? Sparrows?

His words were recorded
by reporters
and microfiched in libraries.

I saw a film praising
the two-time president and 5-star general
for his courage to speak
and thought it ridiculous.

Give the guy credit for D-Day,
but his farewell address was like
if Jesus had said at Gethsemane,
"Father, instead of being crucified,
I just say Satan is bad, okay?"

Eisenhower's conscience, like Oppenheimer's
and ours, is a dreaded glowing
that can never be buried deep enough
to avoid leaching into groundwater.

They Will Find You

There are red-tailed hawk songs,
orange poppies,
and leaping steelhead
below footpaths
thousands of years old

broken by a numbered
sapling-like spaghetti tag,
"ODFW The Dalles,"
unstuck from another fish's
olive back

like a splinter
removed from my thumb
or a bar code scraped
from the sole
of my ragged boot.

Someday,
when this system is over,
glaciers and starshine
will trump every construct
of the human mind.

River Reflections

Like the elk
my vote
won't be heard.

I have little
economic
or political power.

I'm uninterested
in matters
lacking soul.

I gave up
television
when I was 15.

I am a nonessential
and unproductive
worker

yet a threat
to the machine
merely by resting

and thinking.

Here at the End, I Remember

a kid bored out of his mind
changing commas into hawks
and quadratic equations
into dolphins.

Once, he received detention
for attaching doughy cinnamon
elephant ears
to garden saints.

That day, even the old priest
laughed
before scolding him.

What was more important?

Grammar?

Math?

Another solemn garden?

Acknowledgments

Artists' Milepost Art Show, Unnatural Acts: Crimes Against Mother Nature,
"Antarctic Dream After Watching *Chasing Ice*" (Portland, November 2013)

Blast Furnace: "Antarctic Dream After Watching *Chasing Ice*"

Blueline (at SUNY Potsdam): "Here at the End, I Remember"

Blue Lotus Review: "Hiking the Superstitions I Realized"

Cream City Review: "The Dream of Greece, Wisconsin, and One-armed Trees"

Elohi Gadugi Journal: "The Biker on the Ferry from Coupeville to Port Townsend"

Fogged Clarity: "For Uncle Ed"

The Foster Collective's Landslide Gallery Show, "Gulf Oil Disaster Response"
(Chicago, July/August 2010), which featured art and words on gas station
paper towels: "Louisiana Agates"

heartjournalonline.com: "The Other History or How Federal and California
Politicians Killed Indians"

Moksha Journal: "Before You Were Born"

Niche Magazine: "Patient Y"

Nisqually Delta Review: "Thinking About Global Warming and the
Orange Tree Outside My Kitchen Window"

OccuPoetry: "Deep in the Old Growth Forest," "Listening to a Banker Talk
About Losing [Only] Two Billion Dollars as Schools Are Closed,"
"San Diego Swap Meet"

Pemmican: "Moon and Money Poem"

Poets for Living Waters: "Louisiana Agates"

Rune (at Massachusetts Institute of Technology): "The Builders' Sons Discuss
History and Literature"

South 85: "On the Ferry Between Port Angeles and Victoria"

Wild Earth: "And They Thought We Were Talking About Caribou"

Work Literary Magazine: "Ode to Milton Shinklebauer"

*Cover photo, "Dead duck mired in a five acre pond filled with acid water oil
and acid clay sludge," by Bruce McAllister (from the series DOCUMERICA:
The Environmental Protection Agency's Program to Photographically Document
Subjects of Environmental Concern, compiled 1972-1977); cover and interior book
design by Diane Kistner (dkistner@futurecycle.org); Arial Narrow text with Arial
Black titling*

About FutureCycle Press

FutureCycle Press is dedicated to publishing lasting English-language poetry and flash fiction books, chapbooks, and anthologies in both print-on-demand and ebook formats. Founded in 2007 by long-time independent editor/publishers and partners Diane Kistner and Robert S. King, the press incorporated as a nonprofit in 2012. A number of our editors are distinguished poets and writers in their own right, and we have been actively involved in the small press movement going back to the early seventies.

The FutureCycle Poetry Book Prize and honorarium is awarded annually for the best full-length volume of poetry we publish in a calendar year. Introduced in 2013, our Good Works projects are devoted to issues of universal significance, with all proceeds donated to a related worthy cause. Our Selected Poems series highlights contemporary poets with a substantial body of work to their credit. Our flash fiction line presents quick reads that can be serious or light-hearted, irreverent or quirky, fantastic or futuristic, or just plain fun.

We are dedicated to giving all of the authors we publish the care their work deserves, making our catalog of titles the most diverse and distinguished it can be, and paying forward any earnings to fund more great books.

We've learned a few things about independent publishing over the years. We've also evolved a unique, resilient publishing model that allows us to focus mainly on vetting and preserving for posterity the most books of exceptional quality without becoming overwhelmed with bookkeeping and mailing, fundraising activities, or taxing editorial and production "bubbles." To find out more about what we are doing, come see us at www.futurecycle.org.

www.ingramcontent.com/pod-product-compliance
Lightning Source LLC
Chambersburg PA
CBHW060044050426
42448CB00012B/3122